Yesterday on Delaware Avenue

Marjorie G. McNinch

Wilmington, Delaware

First Edition   Yesterday on
                 Delaware
                 Avenue

Published by: Cedar Tree Books, Ltd.
                208 E. Ayre Street
                Wilmington, De 19804
                books@ctpress.com
                www.cedartreebooks.com

ISBN 978-1-892142-31-3

Title: Yesterday on Delaware Avenue
Author: Marjorie G. McNinch
Editor: Beverly Cerchio
Book Design and Layout: Bob Schwartz

Library of Congress Cataloging-in-Publication Data

McNinch, Marjorie G.
  Yesterday on Delaware Avenue / by Marjorie G. McNinch. -- 1st ed.
    p. cm.
  Includes bibliographical references.
  ISBN 978-1-892142-31-3 (alk. paper)
 1. Delaware Avenue (Wilmington, Del.) 2. Historic buildings--Delaware--Wilmington. 3. Wilmington (Del.)--Buildings, structures, etc. 4. Wilmington (Del.)--History. I. Title.

F174.W775D456 2006
975.1'2--dc22

                        2006037008

Copyright © 2006 Cedar Tree Books, Ltd.

All rights reserved. No part of this book may be used, reproduced or transmitted in any form without written permission of the author and the publisher, except in the case of brief quotations embodied in critical essays and reviews.
Printed and bound in the United States of America on 60# archival, acid-free paper meeting the requirements of the American Standard for Permanence of paper for printed Library Materials.

Yesterday on Delaware Avenue

DEDICATION

This book is dedicated to my brothers and sisters: Wilbur, Jr.; George; Carolyn; Dot; Nancy; and Steve, Sr. We all have fond memories of life along the Avenue.

INTRODUCTION

At the close of the year 2005 the fifteen-story Wilmington Savings Fund Society Financial Center was under construction on 1.8 acres of land at 500 Delaware Avenue between Jefferson and Madison Streets. The building, which will house the main offices of the Wilmington Savings Fund Society, the U.S. Post Office and many other offices and businesses, faces the former site of one of two flatiron buildings in the City of Wilmington, Delaware.[1] Building projects like this are nothing new for the Avenue.

Delaware Avenue has seen numerous buildings come and go, as well as reconfigurations of the Avenue itself during its history from 1832, when Wilmington was chartered as a city, to the twenty-first century. Gone is the grand mansion of Job Jackson, of Jackson & Sharp railroad car builders, at Delaware Avenue and Washington Street, which stood where the central YMCA is located today. Gone are the Little Heel, the Kozy Korner, the Purple Door and Smith and Keil Liquors, razed to make way for a hotel at Delaware Avenue and Washington Street. Gone are Wilmington High School, the A&P, the Baltimore & Ohio Railroad Station, the car barn, Bethany Baptist Church, and the Ritz movie theater. The widening of Delaware Avenue in 1916 and the placement of the I-95 expressway through Wilmington in 1968 at Jackson and Adams Streets were responsible for the disappearance of some of these buildings of yesterday. Not all of the buildings which played a part in the Avenue's history have been torn down. The New Century Club is now the Delaware

---

[1] Maureen Milford, "Law Firm to move to new high rise," *The News Journal*, Wilmington, DE, Feb. 1, 2005, p. V7; Adam Taylor, "Post office to open in new tower", *The News Journal*, June 16, 2006, p. B3

Children's Theatre. The second flatiron building between Clayton and DuPont Streets still stands, housing businesses active in what currently is known as Trolley Square. Kelly's Logan House, a National Historic Landmark, thrives as a local tavern at the site on which it was built in 1865. Many fine Victorian homes still line Delaware Avenue, thanks to the efforts of the Delaware Avenue Community Association. Although Delaware Avenue continues to change, it remains rooted in the past.

Yesterday on Delaware Avenue is the story of a thoroughfare which embraced the many immigrants moving into Wilmington by developing farmland into residential and business sectors and creating neighborhoods such as Forty Acres, McDowellville, and the Highlands. Delaware Avenue became a hub for the railroad and provided a home away from work with areas for relaxation and recreation. The following account of life along Delaware Avenue will be nostalgic for some residents and news to the more transient inhabitants. It does not attempt to be all encompassing, but will endeavor instead to present an interesting history of a thoroughfare ever changing.

Table of Contents

Introduction vii

Chapter One . . . . .Early History 3

Chapter Two . . . . .Downtown 29

Chapter Three . . . . .Van Buren to Clayton 65

Chapter Four . . . . .Clayton to Union Streets 85

Chapter Five . . . . .Union to Greehill Avenue .97

Acknowledgements 105

Bibliography 106

Yesterday on Delaware Avenue

Marjorie G. McNinch

Chapter One
Early History

Settlement on land that would become part of Wilmington began in the mid-seventeenth century. The Swedes settled at Fort Christina in 1638. In 1655 the Dutch captured this settlement of about 1,000 persons adding 900 Dutch colonists to the population. The Dutch renamed it Fort Altena, and the small town of Christianham was built up. Christianham was captured by the English in 1664 who let it go to ruin. Between 1664 and 1731 no attempt was made to establish another settlement here.[2]

The territory which is now the City of Wilmington was land granted to John Anderson Stallcap (Johan Anderson) of New Sweden in 1664 and to Tymen Stidham in 1671. Anderson sold half of his land lying on the Christina River to Samuel Peterson in 1675; Peterson's son Peter inherited the land and sold it to Andrew Justison in 1727. Justison's daughter Catherine married Thomas Scott, and after his death she married Thomas Willing of Philadelphia in 1728. In September 1731 Willing's father-in-law Justison assigned land along the Christina River between French and West to Willing, who then proceeded to lay out a town plan similar to that of Philadelphia's, on a grid pattern. He named his town Willingtown. His settlement did not prosper until William Shipley (1693-1768) and his wife Elizabeth moved there from Ridley, Pennsylvania in 1735. With his wealth Shipley purchased

---

[2]Marjorie G. McNinch, <u>Festivals</u> (Wilmington, DE: The Cedar Tree Press, Inc. 1966) p. 9;
J. Thomas Scharf, <u>History of Delaware, 1609-1888</u>, Vol. 2 (Philadelphia: L.G. Richards & Co., 1888), p. 630

acreage from Justison and Willing, and expanded the settlement north to Seventh Street, west to Tatnall Street and east to Walnut Street. In 1739 Great Britain's King George II granted a charter creating the Borough of Wilmington. He changed the name from Willingtown to Wilmington as a favor to his friend Spencer Compton, Earl of Wilmington.[3] Wilmington at this time was a part of Christiana Hundred, but growth in population and industry would change that.

Wilmington's growth was prompted by the Quakers who settled here, encouraged initially to come to the area because of the Penn Charter and because of Wilmington's waterways. William Shipley was instrumental in this development followed by the Gilpins, Tatnalls, Canbys and Leas. These men began enterprises along the Brandywine River, which gradually attracted more people and businesses to the area. By 1814 flour, grist, paper and saw mills lined the shores of the Brandywine River.[4] Six turnpikes ran through New Castle County at this time, assuring Wilmington its place as the county's commercial center. The Wilmington and Kennett Turnpike was chartered on January 21, 1811 to run north and west from Wilmington to the rich farmlands of the Brandywine Valley. It entered Wilmington near Kennett Road (Delaware Avenue) at Old King's Road (Adams Street) and continued north on what is now Pennsylvania Avenue.[5] The du Ponts were responsible for the maintenance of this road over which they transported their gunpowder. The earliest toll gate was at McDowellville which was situated between Pennsylvania and Delaware Avenues at the point where the railroad tracks would cross overhead in the 1880s on Pennsylvania Avenue. Another stopping place on the Wilmington & Kennett Turnpike for farmers bringing their livestock into Wilmington was a hotel called Cross Keys with stabling for the horses and grounds for the cattle. It was noted as a "famous resort at the corner of Delaware Avenue and Adams Street… It was the assembling place for men who were fond of good horses, of racing and shooting, men who talked sport, who were as fond of good liquor as they were of good races." The Wilmington and Kennett Turnpike closed as a toll road in 1919.

---

[3] Anna T. Lincoln, Wilmington, DE: Three Centuries Under Four Flags, 1609-1937 (Rutland, VT: The Tuttle Publishing Company, 1937) pp. 67-73; Scharf, Delaware, pp. 631,636

[4] Marjorie G. McNinch, Bridges (Wilmington, DE: The Cedar Tree Press, Inc. 1995), p. 5

[5] Lincoln, Wilmington, Delaware, pp. 223-223;
Marjorie G. McNinch, Bridges, p. 7;
no author, "The Passing of the Old Kennett Pike," Every Evening, Wilmington, DE, p. 5 from Accession 1410 Box 63, Hagley Museum and Library

The three main ethnic groups who moved to Wilmington in significant numbers in the early 1800s are those who have consistently comprised the higher percentage of the city's foreign born population: they are the English, Irish and German.[6] By 1830 Wilmington's residents called for a new charter, and on February 10, 1832 Wilmington was incorporated as a city, no longer a borough of Christiana Hundred. On January 25, 1833 Wilmington Hundred was erected by act of assembly and called the City of Wilmington. Wilmington's first mayor was Richard H. Bayard (1796-1868), son of James A. Bayard (1767-1815), signer of the Treaty of Ghent. Change was in the wind.[7]

Wilmington's street plan was one of the first changes enacted by the city. In 1835 the old names of streets running parallel to the Christina River were changed to numbers: High Street became Fourth; Queen Street, Fifth; Hanover Street, Sixth; Broad Street, Seventh; Kent Street, Eighth; Wood Street, Ninth; Chestnut Street, Tenth; Elizabeth Street, Thirteenth; Washington Street, Fourteenth; and Stidham Street, Fifteenth. In 1844 Wilmington was divided into five wards with Market and Fourth Streets serving as dividers. The boundaries of Wilmington at this time were the Brandywine and Christina Rivers, Old King's Road (Adams Street) and Lancaster Road (Front Street). King's Roads were all those over which the mail was carried in Colonial times. Adams Street to Delaware Avenue was called a King's Road as late as 1861.[8] Until 1815 Delaware Avenue was called Kennett Road which was an extension of the Brandywine Walk, a stretch of land from Tenth and Market Streets northward. By 1847 Franklin Street became the western boundary, Broom Street in 1861, then Union Street in 1873, and in 1885 Greenhill Avenue became the final boundary. City streets were controlled by the borough until 1832, between 1832 and 1887 by the City Council, and after that by the Wilmington Street and Sewer Department.[9] The railroads would make an impact on the city in the period following the Civil War by allowing people to live away from their work. With the help of enterprising businessmen, residential neighborhoods with supportive services expanded along Delaware Avenue.

---

[6] Marjorie G. McNinch, *Festivals*, p. 11

[7] Lincoln, *Wilmington, Delaware*, p. 236;
Scharf, *Delaware*, P. 640

[8] Lincoln, *Wilmington, Delaware*, pp. 216, 237-238

[9] Mary Ann Barnard, *A History of Forty acres to 1910: Myth and Reality in a Wilmington, Delaware neighborhood* (Newark, DE: University of Delaware, 1981), p. 29;
Henry C. Conrad, *History of the State of Delaware from the earliest settlements to the year 1907* (Wilmington, DE: Author, 1907), pp. 301, 308;
Lincoln, *Wilmington, Delaware*, pp. 216, 220-221

Wilmington in 1832 was a city of 18,000 whose industries were concentrated along the Brandywine and Christina Rivers. Shipbuilding, brick making, tanning and paper manufacture were concentrated in the city. The DuPont Gunpowder Works, established in 1802 north of the city, was bringing in a concentration of Irish as their workforce. The Joseph Bancroft and Sons textile mills and James Riddle's cotton manufacturing concerns were both located south of the DuPont works near where Rattlesnake Run at DuPont Street enters the Brandywine. The land east of Market Street was flat and marshy, and rows of two-story houses were built for the working class in this factory district. The textile workers and powder men all lived in housing provided by their employers. Transportation for these low and middle income workers was limited to foot travel, horse, or wagon. For the workers on the west side of the city, the terrain was steep and rocky. For workers on both the east and west sides of Market Street, living where one worked was a necessity in 1832.[10]

Wilmington's population in 1855 had grown to 20,000 and by 1870 to 30,000. Between 1820 and 1880 over ten-million immigrants, mostly from northwestern Europe, arrived in America, many by way of New York and Philadelphia. As more immigrants settled in Wilmington, the Irish became an important labor force in the iron and steel industry; the British worked as businessmen and manufacturers; and the Germans found their niche in the brewing business, the building trades, and in leather manufacture. The influx of immigrants created a demand for housing, but limited means of transportation encouraged these workers to live near their countrymen in established areas of the city. Enter Joshua T. Heald (b. 1821), Wilmington businessman, who introduced the horse trolley line and developed real estate along Delaware Avenue, away from the city's industry. The land between the Wilmington & Kennett Turnpike, the Brandywine River, and Clayton and Union Streets was owned by the Shallcross and Lovering families, and was known as the Hope Farm. Joseph Shallcross, a wealthy Wilmington Quaker merchant, purchased the property that would comprise his farm in about 1750. He willed his property to his daughter, Mary, and his two sons, John and Isaac. Mary, who married Samuel Lovering, a ship captain, eventually came into possession of the Hope Farm, about 153 acres. Bordering the Shallcross farm were the Gilpin Paper Mills,

---

[10] Carol E. Hoffecker, <u>Wilmington, Delaware: Portrait of an Industrial City, 1830-1910</u> (Virginia: University Press of Virginia for the Eleutherian Mills-Hagley Foundation, 1974), p.37;
Mary Ann Barnard, <u>Forty Acres</u>, p. 49;
Marjorie G. McNinch, <u>Festivals</u>, p. 54

bought and operated by James Riddle in 1838, and the Rockford textile mills of Joseph Bancroft which opened in 1831. In 1815, a proposed road that traveled diagonally across Hope Farm toward what would be the Rockford Works became the present-day Delaware Avenue.[11]

When Mary Lovering died in 1848, the property was still farmland now in possession of her son Joseph and daughter Sarah. Wilmington factory owners and farmers with crops to haul took advantage of railroads running north and east of the city, bypassing Wilmington. Joshua Heald's vision of Wilmington as a commercial center included the Hope Farm as a prime location for a major railroad terminus. Joseph S. Lovering bought out his sister's share of the farm in 1850 for $15,000 and added acreage to increase it to 162 acres. Joseph Lovering, who eventually purchased acreage over to Adams Street, did not live on Hope Farm but in Philadelphia where he was a sugar merchant. By 1861 the Hope Farm was within the city limits, and Heald and James Bradford (b. 1823), founder of the Bradford Paint Company, were on the brink of transforming into reality their vision of Wilmington as a great rail terminus and industrial center incorporating the Lovering property.[12]

The vision of railroad lines running through Wilmington was not a new one. The Philadelphia, Wilmington and Baltimore Railroad had established a line through the east side of the city by 1848. In 1860 a group of businessmen not involving Heald or Bradford proposed the Wilmington and Brandywine Railroad line which would run north along the Brandywine to Rattlesnake Run (DuPont Street) and cross Delaware Avenue at Riddle Road, right through the heart of Hope Farm, Joseph S. Lovering's property. The Wilmington and Brandywine Railroad received its charter on March 5, 1861, but plans were interrupted by the Civil War. On February 7, 1866 the company was renamed the Delaware and State Line Railroad which merged with the Berks and Chester County Railroad on March 16, 1866; the combined company became the Wilmington and Reading Railroad on April 23, 1866. Heald, Bradford, William Gilles, Joseph Tatnall, Edward Betts and Francis Barry were the new company's directors. The route through Lovering's property had been dropped.[13]

During the Civil War Joshua Heald was busy buying up tracts of land, particularly acreage belonging to Joseph S. Lovering and the Hope Farm estate. On May 20, 1863

---

[11] *Historical and Biographical Encyclopedia of Delaware* (Delaware, 1882), p. 564; Mary Ann Barnard, Forty Acres, pp. 9-15, 49

[12] Barnard, <u>Forty Acres</u>, p. 18; <u>Encyclopedia</u>, p. 114

[13] Barnard, <u>Forty Acres</u>, pp. 29-30

Heald, who was Sarah Lovering's attorney, called in the mortgage she held on her brother's property, thus taking control of the Hope Farm property. Heald was, therefore, designated the land agent "for the division and sale of lots" from the original Shallcross property, 176 acres. On March 23, 1864 Lovering disposed of most of his farm property to Heald and William Tatnall. The two bought from Lovering a tract of about forty acres for $15,000; it was located north and west of Delaware Avenue and stretched from Riddle Road to what would become Union Street near the Riddle Mills on the Brandywine. This tract was only about one-quarter of the Hope Farm property. Heald conceptualized the development of lots of this real estate through the formation of the Wilmington City Railway. He visualized prestigious housing along Delaware Avenue, and knew that only dependable transportation would bring the buyers to settle on his route.[14]

In vogue in northern cities in the 1860s were horse-drawn passenger cars on iron rails. Wilmington's only railroad station terminated at Front Street, so Heald formed the Wilmington City Railway Company to start from the Philadelphia, Wilmington & Baltimore Railroad's terminal. On February 4, 1864, a month before the purchase of Lovering's property, the Wilmington City Railway Company was incorporated by the Delaware Legislature. The original directors were Joshua Heald, (President); Philip McDowell, (Vice President); Clement B. Smyth (Secretary & Treasurer); William Tatnall; William Wharton, Jr.; Daniel Bates; and Eli Garrett. Tracks were laid from Front and Walnut Streets, up Market Street to Tenth and out Delaware Avenue past the Shallcross property to Riddle Road (DuPont Street) for a distance of two miles.

William Wharton, Jr., of Philadelphia was awarded the contract of laying the rails for about $30.000. The first car on the line ran on June 30, 1864; and throughout the summer horse cars ran at ten-minute intervals, carrying 1,500 persons a day averaging $90 in daily receipts. The City Railway carried 450,000 passengers its first year of service. The fare was six cents one-way with twenty tickets for a dollar. The line terminated at the Middle Depot on the north side of Delaware Avenue between Riddle Road (DuPont Street) and Clayton Streets. A waiting room, car barn and office comprised the Depot. The line was extended to Union Street, south to Seventeenth Street and west to Rising Sun Village on October 14, 1864. Up to 1880 no extensions were built and no dividends paid. The residential area along the railway's Delaware Avenue route developed as Heald hoped it would for Wilmington's rich, attracting owners such as Job H. Jackson, William Spruance, and Edward Gilpin who built

---

[14]Barnard, *Forty Acres*, pp. 30-33

their mansions along the Avenue, making the route to the Middle Depot the most prestigious in Wilmington before the turn of the twentieth century.[15]

Wharton, the Philadelphia railway builder who had completed the Wilmington City Railway tracks, was also an investor in real estate along Delaware Avenue at Riddle Road. On January 2, 1865 he bought three tracts from Heald and Tatnall, one of them being the northwest section at Delaware Avenue and Riddle Road. It was on this land that he built a hotel later known as the Logan House in honor of Union Commander John Alexander Logan. William Aiken, a carpet weaver, purchased land from Joseph Lovering in 1860 and 1861. Some of this land Aiken sold to Heald and Tatnall on March 18, 1864 for $800. The property was located on the east side of Riddle Road (DuPont Street), and north of Delaware Avenue. It was here that the Middle Depot was built. Tatnall sold this land to the City Railway Company for $1,000. Mr. Aiken remained owner of half the block between Clayton Street, Riddle Road, Delaware and Gilpin Avenues as late as 1876.[16]

By 1888 electric car lines were introduced along the route of the Wilmington City Railway, and horse-drawn cars were replaced by electric ones. A blizzard in 1888 disabled the line, but by late March 1888 the cars began regular service. A waiting room was initially opened at the Ebbitt House at Tenth and Market.[17] The first electric car to run on the Delaware Avenue line was in August 1891. The spur from DuPont Street via Delaware Avenue, Union and Seventeenth Streets out to Rising Sun remained horse-drawn until October 1892 when it was electrified. Through cars to Rising Sun, however, did not operate on the spur until October 1896 when a small waiting station was built. In 1901 the waiting

---

[15] Harold E. Cox, Diamond State Trolleys (Forty Fort, PA: Harold E. Cox, 1991), p. 5;
Barnard, Forty Acres, pp. 33-34, 51;
Hoffecker, Industrial City, pp. 39-40;
Every Evening, History of Wilmington (New York: Press of Moss Engraving Company, 1894), pp. 46, 48;
H. Clay Reed, editor, A History of the First State, (New York: Lewis Historical Publishing Company, Inc., 1947), Vol. 2, p. 525;
Norman B. Wilkinson, The Brandywine Home Front during the Civil War, 1861-1865 (Wilmington, DE: Kaumagraph Company, 1966), pp. 141-142

[16] Barnard, Forty Acres, pp. 56-57;
Scharf, Delaware, Vol. 2, p. 669

[17] Cox, Trolleys, pp. 5, 6, 56-57

station was moved to Rockford Park.[18] By 1900 the City Railway was operating seventy-two electric cars on its twenty-five mile route.

Joshua Heald's land development did not end with the development of the large houses along Delaware Avenue. Just as he had envisioned a prestigious neighborhood along the railway, he also recognized the need for more housing at workers' prices to accommodate Wilmington's swelling population which had reached 30,000 by 1870. As mentioned earlier, Heald and Tatnall bought forty acres of the Lovering tract to the west of Riddle Road in March 1864. The plots of land along Delaware Avenue between Adams and Rodney Streets went the depth of the block from Delaware Avenue to Gilpin Avenue, about 300 feet. The plots to the west of Rodney Street became smaller; none extended the entire block. Heald and Tatnall were involved in land speculation with the goal of turning a profit. With the terminus of the City Railway line extending beyond Riddle Road, the availability of smaller plots for workers in the area's businesses and factories drew in residents to the west of the Logan House. Most of the Heald and Tatnall land, plus smaller tracts owned by others, such as Aiken, Wharton, William Scott, Thomas Taylor and Andrew Hughes, were sold by 1866.[19]

Scott, Taylor and Hughes were small businessmen as well as tradesmen on Delaware Avenue. William Scott owned a house on the southwest corner of Delaware Avenue and what would become Union Street in 1860. On his property he ran a quarry, which operated into the early 1900s. His employees lived in the neighborhood that became known as Forty Acres.

Thomas Taylor and Andrew Hughes purchased land which comprised the block of what would be Gilpin Avenue, Shallcross Avenue, DuPont and Scott Streets. Hughes was a stonecutter, and later a quarry man, who owned about three-quarters of the block on which he built a farm house. His property was bought by the Baltimore & Ohio Railroad when it went through in the 1880s. Taylor, a carpet weaver listed in the 1870 census as owning $1,000 of real estate in this block, also sold his property to the railroad. As more people moved to land along Delaware Avenue, particularly DuPont powder workers and textile workers and their families, the need for regular

---

[18] William F. Rupp, "Notes on Delaware Street and Interurban Railways 1900-1912", The Railway History Monograph (Crete, Nebraska: J-B Publishing Company, 1974), Vol. III, No. 2, p. 18;
Cox, Trolleys, pp. 56-57;
Wilkinson, Home Front, p. 141
[19] Barnard, Forty Acres, pp. 52, 56

transportation increased.[20]

Wilmington of the 1880s had two horse car lines, a new electric line, and five steam railroads. The Wilmington and Reading Railroad went bankrupt in 1877, but was re-chartered and prospered as the Wilmington and Northern Railroad. The Wilmington and Western Railroad, launched by Heald in 1860, lost money and Heald dropped out of sight. James Bradford, a Wilmington City Council member, took Heald's place with the railroad which went into receivership in 1876. William Canby bought the failing railroad for $5,000, and it became the Delaware and Western. In 1883 the Baltimore and Ohio Railroad bought out the Delaware and Western and completed a line through Wilmington along the edge of Forty Acres in December 1884. This placed Forty Acres on the other side of the tracks from the easterly, more grand section of[21] the Lovering property along Delaware Avenue. The City Railway was acquired by the du Ponts by 1910, after the DuPont Company built their headquarters between Tenth and Eleventh Streets on Market, and was renamed the Wilmington and Philadelphia Traction Company. This company was sold to Van Horn Ely of Pittsburgh in 1914, and in 1915 it merged with the Peoples Railway, which had started operations out of Sixth Street in June 1901. The Wilmington and Philadelphia Traction Company was renamed the Delaware Electric Power Company in 1927. By the 1930s transportation systems in Wilmington were converting to trackless trolleys with the implementation of electric lines, and the Delaware Avenue line was converted in 1938. The Delaware Electric Power Company changed its name to the Delaware Coach Company in 1941. By 1957 the trackless electric transit system was history.

Such was the history of the transportation lines along Delaware Avenue, bringing residential development to the area that was once farmland and invigorating a downtown business center at Rodney Square on Market between Tenth and Eleventh Streets. Since 1864, when the first horse-drawn car traveled along Delaware Avenue, that thoroughfare has seen constant growth and change. Wilmington directories tell us what buildings, businesses, and people shared space along its route. Memories passed down in pictures and words, however, reveal a more colorful story.

---

[20]Barnard, *Forty Acres*, pp. 56-58;
McNinch, *Festivals*, pp. 13, 54
[21]Barnard, *Forty Acres*, pp. 36-42;
Cox, *Trolleys*, p. 15;
Lincoln, *Wilmington, Delaware*, p. 232

Aerial view of Delaware Avenue
looking east from Van Buren Street. Ca. 1932.

Dallin Collection
Courtesy Hagley Museum and Library

Map of the City of Wilmington
from D. G. Beers, *Atlas of the State of Delaware*, 1868

Courtesy Hagley Museum and Library

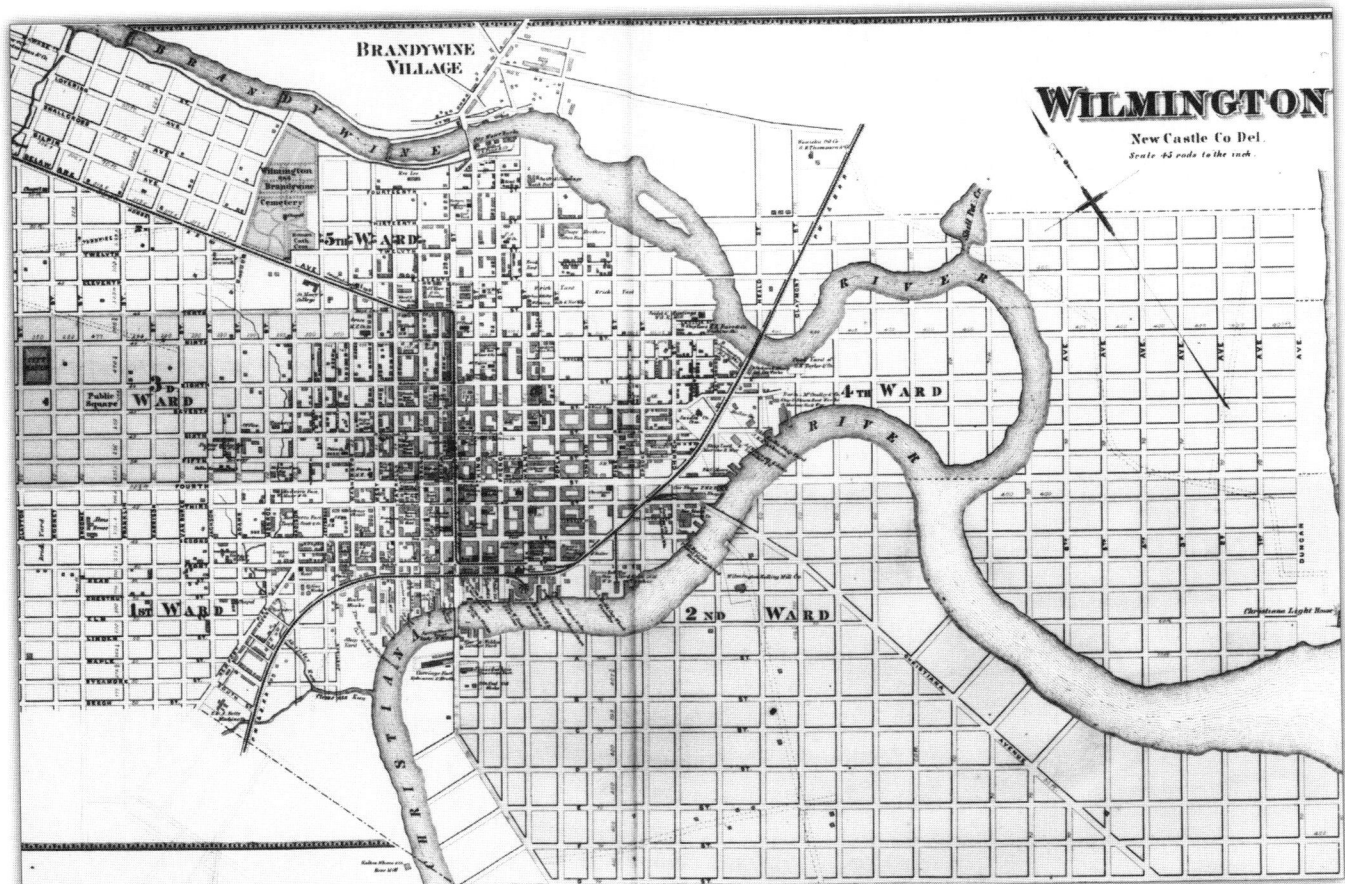

Delaware Avenue with the Wilmington
and Brandywine Cemetery on the left and Wilmington
High School on the right. Ca. 1930.

P. S. du Pont Collection
Courtesy Hagley Museum and Library

Bird's eye view of Wilmington, 1865.

Courtesy Hagley Museum and Library

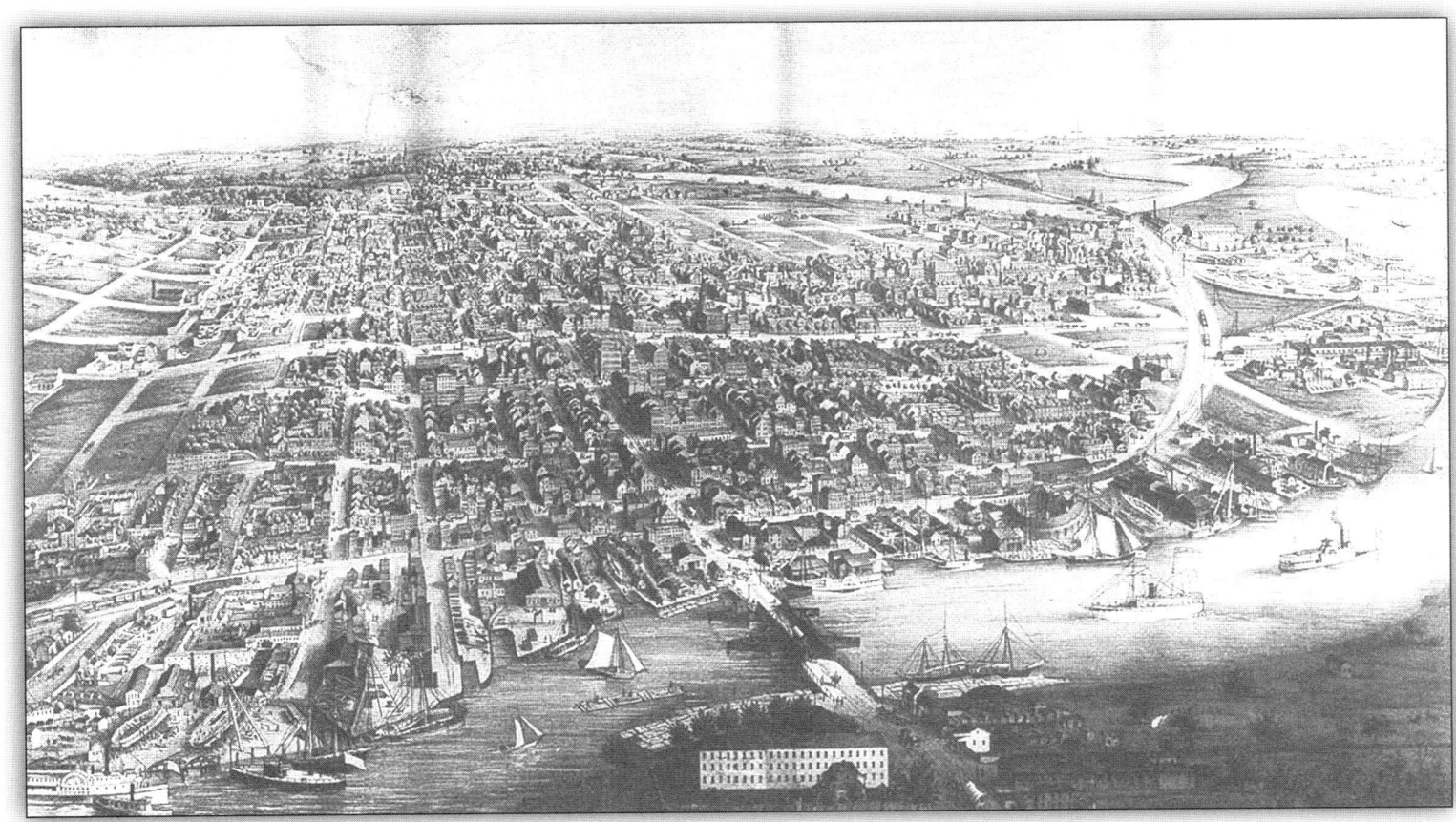

Joshua T. Heald (1821 - 1887). Portrait from
the *Historical and Biographical Encyclopedia of Delaware*
(Wilmington: 1882) opp. P 569.

Courtesy Hagley Museum and Library

Wilmington City Horse Railroad Depot,
or Middle Depot, located at Delaware Avenue
and Du Pont Street. Ca. 1892.

Courtesy Hagley Museum and Library

First electric car seen in front
of Ebbitt Hotel on Market Street between
10th and 11th Streets. Ca. 1892.

P. S. du Pont Collection
Courtesy Hagley Museum and Library

1876 map of Wilmington
showing Delaware Avenue from Market Street
to Union Street being in the 7th Ward.

Courtesy Hagley Museum and Library

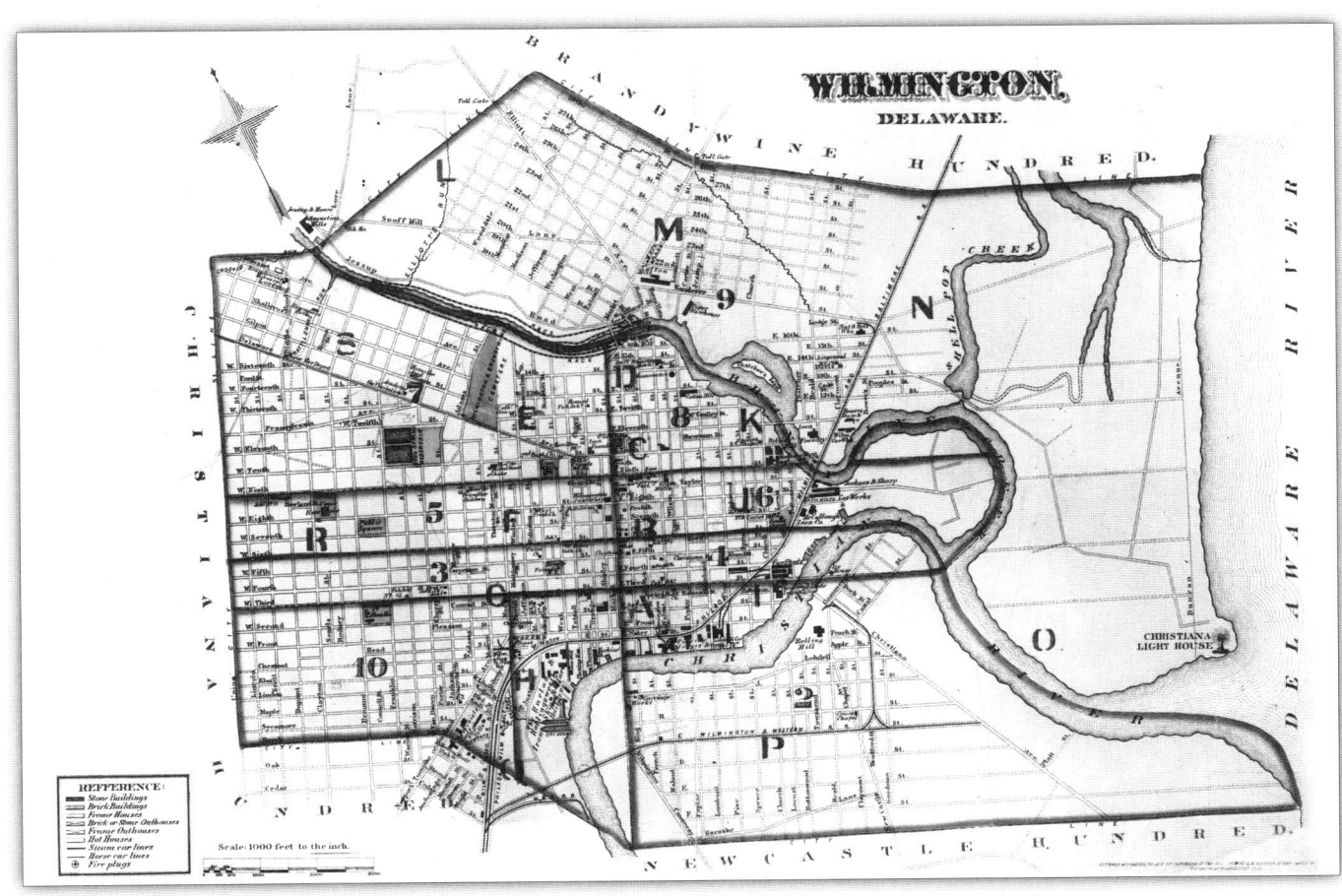

Chapter Two
Downtown

In <u>Reminiscences of Wilmington,</u> which she published in 1851, Elizabeth Montgomery writes of a bull frog pond on the southeast corner of Tatnall Street and Kennett Road that bordered the Bull Frog Tavern. Montgomery refers to the bull frogs as "Les Messieurs," and states what a savory dish one of these frogs made when cooked up. In eloquent prose, Montgomery goes on to say, "Yet they were prosperous…, and when spring put forth its blossoms, they tuned their pipes." The Bull Frog Tavern was just a shanty put up by Billy McDougall, and some youngsters nailed the sign "The Bull Frog Tavern" to his hut. McDougall and the bull frog tribe gave way to industry and mansions on Delaware Avenue.[22]

Downtown Wilmington of 1850 was not yet the business center it would become by 1900, yet Wilmington's entrepreneurs had built mansions along the Avenue on both the north and south sides from Tatnall Street to Old King's Road (Adams Street), the western boundary. Dr. William Gibbons, a prominent citizen who was gifted in the literary arts, built a large mansion in 1820 near the Bull Frog Tavern. Dr. James Tilton (1745-1822) lived farther out the Avenue on the south side near Broom Street in a mansion on farmland he purchased from Bancroft Woodcock; the farm was called Federal Hill. Mr. Woodcock, a silversmith who died of old age around 1820, was known for his ice skating prowess and his love of walking for exercise. Dr. Tilton, who served as Surgeon General of the

---

[22]Elizabeth Montgomery, <u>Reminiscences of Wilmington, In Familiar Villages Tales</u> (Philadelphia: T.K. Collins, 1851), pp. 316-317

U.S. Army in 1812, changed the name of the farm to Tilton Hill, and then to Bellevue. The stone mansion towered so high that it was said that from its heights one could see the steeple of Christ Church in Philadelphia. The Tilton Hospital, which filled the entire block bounded by Ninth Street, Delaware Avenue, Tatnall and West Streets, functioned throughout the Civil War. Moses Bradford had a handsome stone mansion built on the north side. He transformed the 'rugged cornfield' to cultivated grounds with a flourishing garden. On the Avenue between Jefferson and Madison Streets stood St. Mary's, a Roman Catholic College under the directorship of Father Patrick Reilly of St. Peter's Cathedral. The only school for Catholic students in the area before the Civil War, it attracted many pupils who came from a distance to be educated there. A Swedish family headed by John Hedges Sr. lived next to the College.[23]

By the 1840s the Cross Keys Hotel gave way to a finely landscaped new cemetery, the Wilmington and Brandywine, on the north side of the Avenue between Jackson and Madison Streets. The setting of gardens, shrubbery, trees and intertwining paths offered a quiet place for strollers and attracted people to settle in the surrounding area. Mansions started going up along Delaware Avenue from Tatnall to Adams Street. Edward Gilpin (1803-1876), Delaware's Chief Justice, built his house facing the cemetery at Madison. It was razed in 1901 to make way for the massive Wilmington High School. Job H. Jackson, one of the founders of Jackson & Sharp Company, builders of railroad cars, built a stately home in a park-like setting on Delaware Avenue between Washington and Jefferson. This estate was cleared in 1927 for the Young Men's Christian Association (YMCA). By the end of the nineteenth century the Wilmington City Railway impacted the growth of downtown as well as Delaware Avenue to the extent that the city limits were extended to Greenhill Avenue.[24]

Between the Civil War and 1901 downtown Wilmington along Delaware Avenue became the home of the Academy of

---

[23] *Every Evening, Wilmington*, p. 44;
Federal Writers' Project of the Works Progress Administration for the State of Delaware, *Delaware, A Guide to the First State*, American Guide Series, Sponsored by Edward W. Cooch, Lt. Governor (New York: The Viking Press, 1938), p. 313;
Theophilus K. Jones, "Recollections of Wilmington from 1845 to 1860," Chapter 52, Vol. 5, *Historical and Biographical Papers* (Wilmington, DE: Historical Society of Delaware, 1909), pp. 12-13

[24] Hoffecker, *Industrial City*, p. 41;
Gary Mullinax, "Up and Down the Avenue," *Sunday News Journal*, November 10, 1996, pp. C1 & 10

Music, built in 1884 for $30,000 at Delaware Avenue and Tatnall Street. The original building burned in 1888, was rebuilt in 1890, and four years later became the Peoples Theatre. The Walter Mode Carriage Works, Marble Works, Iron Fence Works, Delaware Avenue Baptist Church, Trinity Episcopal Church, the New Jerusalem Temple (Swedenborgian Church), the New Century Club, and the James A. Garfield Monument on an island between Washington and Jefferson were also located on Delaware Avenue. The Delaware Avenue Baptist Church was at Delaware Avenue and West Streets in 1870, having formed in 1865 after members split from the Second Baptist Church. Bethany Baptist Church was organized in 1878 and built a new church at Elm and Jackson Streets in 1888. In 1889 a new chapel and lot were purchased by the Baptist City Mission on Lincoln Street near Delaware Avenue. The New Century Club was founded in 1889 by a group of women seeking to establish intellectual, social and charitable outlets for upper-class women. The club was housed at Delaware Avenue and Jackson Street in a building designed by Mrs. Minerva Parker Nichols of Philadelphia and offered lectures and concerts to the public. The Trinity Protestant Episcopal Church, Rectory and Parish House were built on Delaware Avenue and Adams Street in 1890 after many years at Fifth and King Streets. The turn of the twentieth century brought the DuPont Company downtown, which caused disruption of the businesses and homes there, but also brought a new look to the Avenue.[25]

Pierre S. du Pont had this to say of driving down Delaware Avenue in the 1890s. "No person thought of driving down Delaware Avenue (until 1899 when the first brick pavement was laid) unless the wheels of the carriage were kept upon the rails of the horse cars." The streets were of rough cobblestones. It was not until about 1914 that roads were constructed of tar and asphalt to accommodate the automobile. The DuPont Company, makers of explosives and gunpowder since 1802, moved its headquarters from its works on the Brandywine River in Greenville to Market Street between Tenth and Eleventh. The twelve-story DuPont Building would house the company's staff, and a theater and hotel would also become part of the structure. The first section opened in 1907 and the sixth section, which filled the block, was completed in 1937. Gone was the Ebbitt House, a waiting room for the City Railway; gone were many small houses, the Harkness Building, Philip Wood's Drug Store, and Ginther's Cigar Shop. The new office

---

[25] *Every Evening, Wilmington, pp. 47-48, 129; Baist, 1901;*
Allen J. Henry, Life of Alexis I. duPont (Philadelphia: Wm. F. Fell Co., 1945), pp. 45, 49;
Marjorie G. McNinch, Wilmington In Vintage Postcards (Charleston, SC: Arcadia Publishing, pp. 49, 74

building attracted more people to the city, and they found housing out Delaware Avenue.[26]

The mansions along the Avenue as far as Van Buren Street would succumb to the growth along this thoroughfare. The first estate to go was that of Edward Gilpin across from the Wilmington and Brandywine Cemetery to make room for the new Wilmington High School. Built in 1899, it was the city's first high school, and by 1933 had 4,300 students enrolled. A new Wilmington High School was built on Lancaster Avenue and DuPont Road in 1959, and the sixty-year old school on Delaware Avenue was razed for the construction of the Chase Manhattan Bank building. Next to go was the 1878 mansion of Washington Hastings, president of an iron plate manufactory, at the place between Van Buren and Harrison Streets on Delaware and Pennsylvania Avenues. In 1912 the Kennett Apartments were built there, which were razed for Luther Towers senior housing in 1966. The third mansion to become dust was that of Job H. Jackson at Washington Street and Delaware Avenue. The site became the home of the Young Men's Christian Association (YMCA) in 1928. In a letter between Henry B. du Pont and attorney Christopher L. Ward on November 25, 1927, the selling price of about $261,000 was discussed. In 1912 the city's first flatiron building was built at Delaware Avenue between Madison and Jefferson Streets. It housed the Marion Apartments until 1972 when it was destroyed by fire. A parking lot and an Irish pub took turns on this space, where currently the new WSFS Financial Center is under construction.[27]

Two events on this downtown stretch of Delaware Avenue would alter the configuration of business and residential buildings. In 1913 Pierre S. du Pont (1870-1954), then President of the DuPont Company, decided that he needed to widen Delaware Avenue to facilitate his commute from Longwood Gardens near Hamorton, Pennsylvania, which he purchased in 1906, to his office on Wilmington's Market Street. By 1916 trees lining Delaware Avenue were felled to give way to a wider thoroughfare. The Swedenborgian Church with the James A. Garfield Monument nearby, where Delaware Avenue and Eleventh Street crisscross, were in the way of this street project and had to be moved. The Church, founded in 1824 by Philadelphia cotton manufacturer Daniel Lammot (1782-1877), was moved stone by stone to its present location at Pennsylvania Avenue and Broom Street in 1917, and erected in the

---

[26] Pierre S. duPont essay on life in Wilmington, Del. Longwood Manuscripts Group 10 Series B, Box 1686, pp. 11, 16, 18
[27] McNinch, Postcards, pp. 36, 73;
Mullinax, "Avenue", P. C10;
Letter between Henry B. duPont and Christopher L. Ward, 25 November 1927, Henry B. duPont Papers, Accession 1608 Box 139, Hagley Museum and Library

same form. The statue of James A. Garfield (1831-1881), U.S. President in 1880, was moved to Twenty-third and Jefferson Streets.[28] John J. Raskob (1879-1950), a DuPont Company executive, negotiated with the residents and businesses for P.S. du Pont, which allowed this project to go forth. Businesses which gave up frontage on the Avenue were the Avenue Theatre and the Wilmington Automobile Company, both on Tenth Street. In October 1917 Raskob heard from attorney John D. Nields about the negotiations, who wrote, "I am glad to inform you that the Delaware Avenue project is assured." Raskob also met with the Wilmington Street and Sewer Department to clear the way. There was difficulty in the negotiations with Matthew D. Murphy, owner of the Belvedere Apartments at 1005 Delaware Avenue which lost some frontage, but assurance was made "that he will have only the benefits that will accrue from the betterment of the street." Delaware Avenue was widened twenty feet, from Tatnall to Van Buren Streets reaching a width of seventy-eight and a half feet at a cost to Mr. du Pont of about $300,000.[29] Changes, such as this widening project caused, were always seen as positive in the eyes of most businessmen.

Five years after this street widening, a movie theater was built on Delaware Avenue between Adams and Jackson. The Parkway Theatre with seating for 1,024 persons opened on July 30, 1921. Due to failing attendance, the Parkway was taken over in 1931 by Loew's which reopened with a showing of "Possessed" starring Joan Crawford and Clark Gable. In 1940 the Parkway was the first in Wilmington to show "Gone With the Wind." The following year Loew's and Warner Brothers exchanged theaters and the Parkway became the Ritz. The Ritz enjoyed success on Delaware Avenue until the second restructuring occurred: the building of Interstate 95 through the city starting in 1962, taking with it structures on Adams and Jackson Streets. The final showing at the Ritz Theatre was "Too Late Blues" starring Bobby Darrin and Stella Stevens. Along with The Ritz, the Far East Chinese Restaurant, Smith & Strevig Drugstore, Keil Auto, the Beeson Funeral Home, houses and apartment buildings, and the A&P grocery across from the theater met their demise. Trinity Church survived and still graces the Avenue.[30]

Longtime residents Ruth Kolber and Jean Lyons were pressed by the author to remember what buildings and stores

---

[28] McNinch, Postcards, pp. 44, 123

[29] Letters between John P. Nields and John J. Raskob, 10 & 15 October, 1917, 8 February 1918, 11 & 12 January, 1918, 15, 18 & 29\8 December 1917, John J. Raskob Papers, Accession 473 File 1688, Hagley Museum and Library

[30] Marjorie G. McNinch, Silver Screen (Wilmington, DE: Cedar Tree Books, 1977), pp. 92-97; Mullinax, "Avenue", p. C10

stood in downtown Wilmington along Delaware Avenue between Washington and Tatnall Streets. The No. 2 public school on Eleventh Street opposite the YMCA on the northeast corner made way for the Wilmington Trust Building there. A popular eating place, The Kozy Korner, headed the block with The Purple Door dress shop, The Little Heel, Smith and Keil Liquors, Ellison's Savings & Loan Company, Bird Speakman, Louis Davis Jewelers, a drug store, a men's shoe store, and a radio store. Ruth and Jean frequented these places because in the 1940s and 1950s they were in easy walking distance of their homes or on the bus route. There were also the Martha Washington candy store, Storms' Shoes, and Willard Wilson's TV and radio store nearby. The Medical Arts Building at Delaware Avenue and Jefferson Street housed Brittingham's Pharmacy, later Cutsler's Pharmacy. The 1950s marked the beginning of the shift in population from the city to the suburbs, and with I-95 cutting through downtown in 1968 the exodus was even more pronounced. Downtown stores and movie theaters moved to suburban malls. Today, Delaware Avenue no longer has a movie theater, but in downtown Wilmington banks and hotels thrive along its sidewalks.

10th Street looking towards Delaware Avenue, 1930.

P. S. du Pont Collection
Courtesy Hagley Museum and Library

Delaware Avenue at Jefferson Street
after the widening undertaken by
Pierre S. du Pont (1870 - 1954), 1930.

P. S. du Pont Collection
Courtesy Hagley Museum and Library

Wilmington and Brandywine Cemetery, 1915.

P. S. du Pont Collection
Courtesy Hagley Museum and Library

New Century Club at Jackson Street on Delaware Avenue.
It is now the Delaware Children's Theatre.

Collection of Gordon Pfeiffer

Pierre S. du Pont (1870 - 1954)
and John J. Raskob (1879 - 1950), Ca. 1950.

Courtesy Hagley Museum and Library

Postcard view of the DuPont Building
on Market Street at Rodney Square. Ca. 1930

Author's Collection

The Ebbitt Hotel on Market Street
between 10th and 11th Streets. It had a waiting room
for passengers of the Wilmington City Railway.

P. S. du Pont Collection
Courtesy Hagley Museum and Library

Postcard view of Wilmington High School
on Delaware Avenue. Ca. 1930

Author's Collection

Postcard view of Wilmington's first flatiron building constructed in 1912 as the Marion Apartments. Ca.1915

P. S. du Pont Collection
Courtesy Hagley Museum and Library

Aerial view of Wilmington, Delaware
with Wilmington High School in the foreground, 1929

Dallin Collection
Courtesy Hagley Museum and Library

Delaware Avenue at 11ᵗʰ Street
before the widening of the the Avenue in 1916.
Note the Swedenborgian Church
and the James A. Garfield Monument,
both of which were moved.

P. S. du Pont Collection
Courtesy Hagley Museum and Library

Delaware Avenue and Jackson Street
looking northwest, 1930.

P. S. du Pont Collection
Courtesy Hagley Museum and Library

Looking east toward the city along Delaware Avenue from Jackson Street. The Parkway movie theatre is on the right and the Wilmington and Brandywine Cemetery is on the left.

P. S. du Pont Collection
Courtesy Hagley Museum and Library

Trinity Episcopal Church was built at the corner of
Delaware Avenue and Adams Street in 1882.
It was spared the wrecking ball when the
I-95 expressway cut through the city in 1968.

Collection of Gordon Pfeiffer

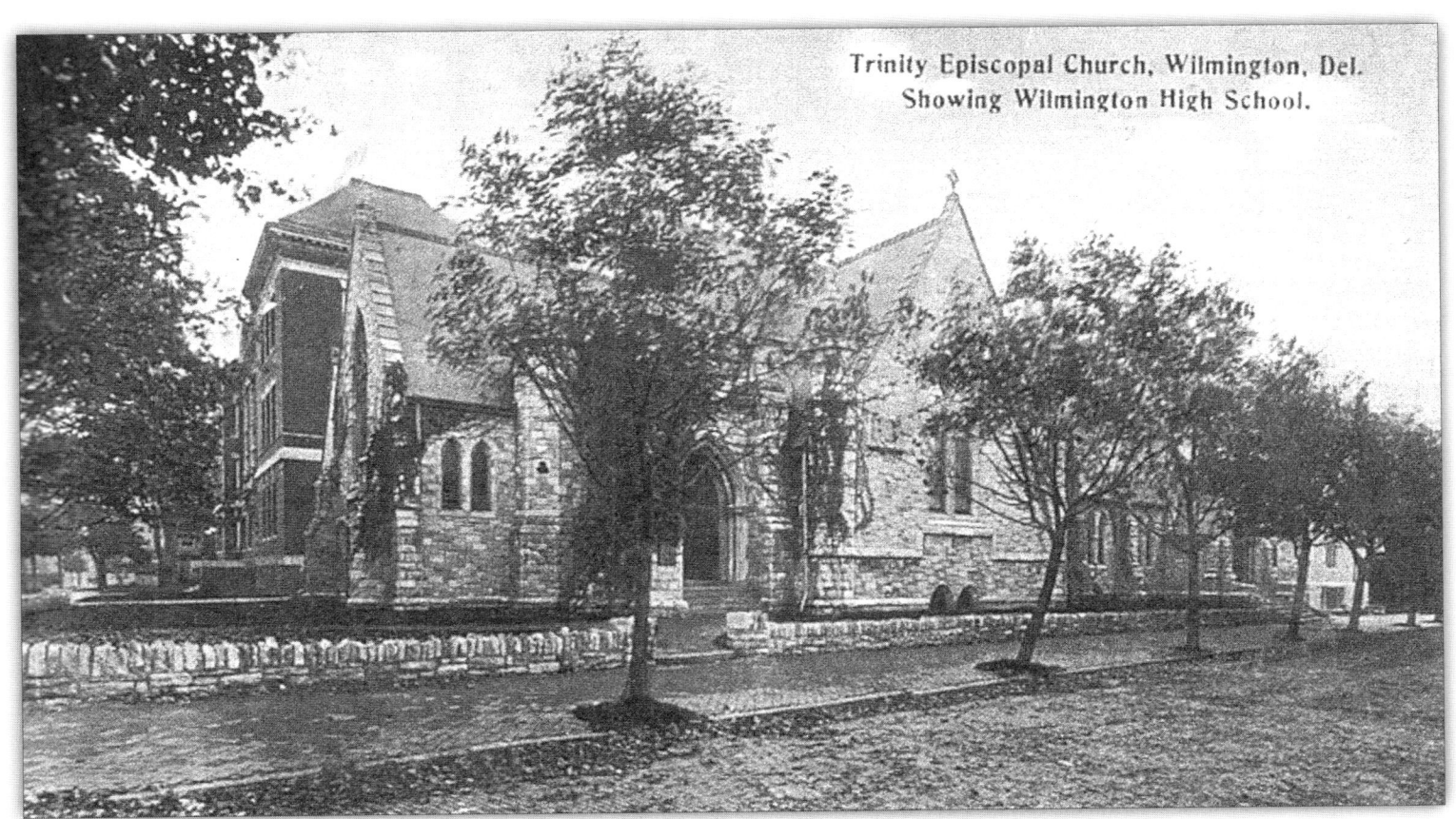

Chapter Three

Van Buren to Clayton

Joshua T. Heald's prestigious neighborhood was showcased by the grand Victorian houses built along Delaware Avenue from Van Buren Street to the Middle Depot of the Wilmington City Railway line. An 1869 broadside advertising 1313 Delaware Avenue promotes it as "the new first-class double residence, one of the most beautiful sites on the Avenue with lawn 50 ft. front by 300 ft. deep planted with ornamental trees." This three-story building boasted fifteen rooms including a parlor, library, dining room, kitchen, and center hall. The broadside continues to advertise the public sale of twelve lots on Delaware Avenue, Fourteenth, Rodney, and Broom Streets. These lots were said to have "the most commanding view of any on the Avenue. With the horse car line passing by "more than 150 times every day" even on Sunday, the property would "be positively sold.[31]

Henry Seidel Canby (1878-1961), whose relative William was instrumental in developing the Avenue, grew up at 1212 Delaware Avenue and remembers the housing in his 1934 book The Age of Confidence. He refers to the houses of the 1870s as brick boxes with cupolas or mansard roofs and porches screened by ornamental iron work. Houses built in the 1880s and 1890s were constructed of green serpentine as well as brick in the pseudo-Gothic style with turrets and pointed towers. The Canby residence was razed in the 1900s for an apartment building built of brick. Next to the Canby residence was the Italianate villa of the Academy of the Visitation, fore-

---

[31]Broadside, 1869 advertisement for the sale of lots on Delaware Avenue, Wilmington, DE, Historical Society of Delaware

runner of the present day Ursuline Academy on Pennsylvania Avenue. The villa was dismantled in the early twentieth century, and the Mayfair Apartments were built on this site. Another Wilmington resident who had his house built across the street from the Canbys in 1872 at 1211 Delaware Avenue was William C. Spruance (b.1831), U.S. Senator and U.S. District Attorney. Jeffries & Sons of Wilmington built his two-story brick house with a mansard roof and a one-story brick back kitchen, between July 1872 and March 1873 for $10,000.[32] "The main building will be 39 feet front and 32 feet deep….The elevation will be precisely the same as William M. Canby's house or $37^{1/2}$ inches." The specifications from cellar to window sills are detailed in the agreement with Jeffries. The landscaping by P. Canberry was $102.30. This wonderful architectural specimen still stands.

The house at 1313 Delaware Avenue advertised in the 1869 broadside was actually purchased by James Johnson, a home furnishings man. At 1311 a house in the Italianate style with a low gabled roof and tall windows was built by a shoemaker's son. Eli Garrett of the Edgemoor Iron Company and his wife once owned the ornately trimmed Gothic revival house at 1315 with arched, pointed windows, a pitched roof, and walls extending to the gables. Mrs. Garrett was one of the presiders over the New Century Club built in the 1880s. The financial panic of the 1890s marked the end of such Victorian grandeur. Continuing along the 1300 block, the house at 1304 is in the Queen Anne Style, built in 1888 by Henry B. Seidel, a Canby relative in the sheet iron business. House 1306, built by the Quigley family, is in the French Empire style with a mansard roof, an oval window in the central dome and louvered shutters. Another Queen Anne at 1308 was built by local attorney Levi Bird in the 1870s. The house was purchased by leather maker William H. Beadenkopf, followed by Col. Edmund Buckner, Vice President of the DuPont Company in 1910.[33]

Delaware Avenue was also home to two other DuPont Company employees. Jasper Elliott Crane, a Vice President of

---

[32] Mullinax, "Avneue", p. C10;
Encyclopedia, p. 545;
Articles of agreement between J. Jeffries & Son and William C. Spruance, 8 July 1872, Spruance/Lea Family Papers, Accession 1114 Item 135, Hagley Museum and Library;
Itemized bill of landscaping done by P. Canberry, 1873, Accession 1114 Item 136, Hagley Museum and Library
[33] Donata Guena, "Walking Back in Time, in Design," The News Journal, Wilmington, DE, 31 December 1992, p.6

the company, lived at 1101. Mr. Crane is documented as having electrical work and painting done there by Wilmington firms in 1919; Garrett, Miller & Company did the electrical work, and Charles Cardwell, the painting. Ten years later Mr. Crane was living in Westover Hills. In 1928 Wallace Carothers, a chemist and teacher at Harvard who had been brought to Wilmington by the DuPont Company as an expert in organic chemistry, lived in an apartment at 1410 Delaware Avenue. Carothers went on to discover NYLON, a product that has had far reaching effects for man and the Du Pont Company.[34]

In 1932 the State Housing Commission reported that the Seventh Ward, which includes Delaware Avenue, showed a thirty per cent increase in population over a period of thirty years. "The central portion of this ward holds many of the large older homes of the City which have been made into apartments" the report continues. Because home ownership in the area is above average, the population in this section of the ward has remained stable. Apartments were not new to the Van Buren-Clayton Street section of Delaware Avenue: three apartment buildings were constructed at Van Buren and Harrison Streets on Delaware Avenue, taking two grand homes in their wake. Artists Howard Pyle, Stanley Arthurs, Frank Schoonover and Gayle Hoskins lived in the neighborhood.. In 1970 Wilmington City Councilman James Baker introduced an ordinance to preserve the 1200-1400 blocks of Delaware Avenue over to Lovering Avenue as an historic district. The Delaware Avenue Community Association is active in maintaining the area's history. Historian Justine Mataleno, past president of the association, lectures on the area at association meetings that are open to the public; this author attended one. In 1979 this group, with the help of local architect Richard Chalfant, had the Frank Schoonover Studios listed on the National Register of Historic Places. Apartment construction in the Seventh Ward has been kept to a minimum and in keeping with the style of the neighborhood.[35]

Following the Civil War there was a desire in Wilmington to erect a monument dedicated to the memory of those who fought and died in that war. In 1869 the Delaware Legislature granted a charter to the Soldiers' and Sailors' Monument Association who selected a triangular site bounded by Broom and Fourteenth Streets and Delaware Avenue. Part of the Lovering

---

[34] Letter, Garrett, Miller & Co. to Jasper E. Crane, 26 September 1919, and itemized bill to Crane from J.A. Montgomery, Jr., 2 November 1927, Jasper E. Crane Papers, Accession 1416 Box 8, Hagley Museum and Library;

Letter, John L. Johnson to Wallace Carothers, 4 October 1928, John L. Johnson Papers, Accession 1842, Hagley Museum and Library

[35] Guena, "Back in Time," p.6

estate, the plot was sold to the association for one dollar by Joshua T. Heald, agent for the estate. The site was deeded to the trustees of the association on June 14, 1879, and on May 30, 1871 the monument was unveiled. It is a tall marble column that was once a pillar in the old Pennsylvania Bank of Philadelphia. Designed by Benjamin Latrobe, the bank was razed in 1868. When the monument was unveiled money was still owed for purchase of the column, and the dedication was nearly halted until a newspaper man, Eli Crozier, raised the funds to pay for it. The bronze eagle killing a serpent on the globe atop the column was molded from a brass cannon donated by Congress in July 1870. The molding was done by Harry Lowe, and it was fashioned at the Pusey & Jones Company in Wilmington. The dedication oration was delivered by General O.O. Howard, the director of the Freedman's Bureau, a federal agency that assisted freed slaves. In 1891 the size of the lot was reduced and the residue was converted into streets and sidewalks. William du Pont paid $1,000 in 1893 to enclose the square base of the monument with granite capping in order to keep it in good condition. The Soldiers' and Sailors' Monument is under the supervision of the Park Commission of Wilmington.[36] The annual Memorial Day parade marches up Delaware Avenue from Greenhill Avenue to the memorial, where a ceremony is held. At the triangle between Delaware and Pennsylvania Avenues near the Canby house, stood another monument, the Ferris Bringhurst Fountain. Bringhurst, a chemist, and the founder of the Wilmington Fountain Society, died in a laboratory explosion in 1871. Erected to his memory in 1872, the fountain was removed in 1965 and was spared from destruction by W.W. 'Chick' Laird (d.1989), who stored it in his barn for twenty years. In 1988 it was placed in the middle of the Jasper Crane Rose Garden in Brandywine Park. It saw new life as a working fountain when it was set in a stone terrace overlooking the Brandywine River next to the garden in 2004.[37]

---

[36] McNinch, Postcards, p. 125;
Every Evening, Wilmington, p. 146;
WPA, Delaware, A Guide, p. 313;
history sheet on the Soldiers' and Sailors' Monument, no date, Accession 1608 Box 61 Historical Society of Delaware file, Hagley Museum and Library
[37] McNinch, Postcards, p. 123;
Robin Brown, "Fountain Sparkles in riverside setting," The News Journal, Wilmington, DE, 13 July 2004

North side of Delaware Avenue
at Jackson Street, 1930.

P. S. du Pont Collection
Courtesy Hagley Museum and Library

Northeast corner of Delaware Avenue
at Van Buren Street. 1930.

P. S. du Pont Collection
Courtesy Hagley Museum and Library

Delaware Avenue looking eastward from
Franklin Street, showing Canby's "brick boxes"
and a wide street, 1890

Courtesy Historical Society of Delaware

These mansions on Broom Street
were typical of ones that lined Delaware Avenue
and Clayton Streets. Ca. 1890.

Collection of Gordon Pfeiffer

Kennett apartments on Delaware Avenue
at Harrison Street, 1930. Luther Towers senior
housing stands there currently.

P. S. du Pont Collection
Courtesy Hagley Museum and Library

Postcard view of the Soldiers' and Sailors' Monument
at Delaware Avenue and Broom Street, 1910.

Courtesy Hagley Museum and Library

Bringhurst Memorial Fountain as it stood
on a triangle where Delaware and Pennsylvania Avenues
split at Van Buren Street, 1910

Collection of Gordon Pfeiffer

Chapter Four
Clayton to Union Streets

This section of Delaware Avenue became a hub of the thoroughfare as soon as the Wilmington City Railway constructed its line out to its terminus at the Middle Depot between Clayton and what became DuPont Street (formerly Riddle Road) after the Civil War. By the end of 1865 William Wharton Jr. had erected a hotel on the northwest corner of DuPont Street opposite the Middle Depot called the Logan House. The City Railway had installed an artificial lake where the Baltimore and Ohio Railroad Station would be built in the 1880s. "Skating is the fashion for young ladies now," remarked Mrs. Henry B. DuPont (Louisa Gerhard, 1816-1900) of her daughter Evelina, who was impressed that due to the mild weather of December 1864 the skating pond did not freeze. Riddle Woods beyond the railway became a favorite picnicking spot during the warmer months. The naturalness of the area, the open fields and woods, made the neighborhood developing as Forty Acres a desirable place to live. Land plots were sold and subdivided, and thus were smaller than the plots on the eastern side above Clayton Street. The houses to the west of the Middle Depot were smaller, less elegant, denser, yet they served the growing community of Irish, German, and English who worked as artisans, stonecutters, mill workers, wagon drivers and laborers.[38] By the end of 1864 fourteen new

---

[38] Barnard, <u>Forty Acres</u>, pp. 73-74;
Wilkinson, <u>Home Front</u>, pp. 142, 144

houses were advertised for sale; two costing over $18,000, a high price. By 1866 Joshua Heald and Henry Tatnall had disposed of their property in the Lovering tract, and the housing boom in Forty Acres moved forward.

Among the most noted landmarks in the City of Wilmington is the Logan House, named for General John Alexander Logan, one of the Union's most formidable commanders. The Logan House was placed on the National Historic Register in 1980. How and why did this establishment survive? It survived because the community it serves continues to need what the tavern has to offer: relaxation, refreshment and entertainment. The Logan House is very much a part of the history of Delaware Avenue, and its owners have taken much pride in its operation. Wharton sold the hotel soon after he built it to Townsend Thompson and his wife for $8,000. In February of 1868 Thompson sold it to a German hotel manager, Sylvester Rianhard for $10,000 who owned and operated it until 1889, when Irish immigrant John David Kelly Sr. and his wife Hannah Golden Kelleher Kelly bought it that September for $15,000. During Rianhard's time the hotel served primarily as a boarding house for cotton mill and DuPont gunpowder workers who were beginning to move into Forty Acres. The Baltimore and Ohio Railroad constructed its depot across the street from the Logan House in 1884 bringing in traveling guests to the tavern which still served as the local gathering place.[39]

John David and Hannah Kelly came to Wilmington in 1880 from County Cork, Ireland. Mr. Kelly, who loved to talk, became a button salesman; his wife worked as a school teacher. Achieving monetary success at selling buttons, Mr. Kelly bought a tavern at Water and Market Streets. Not long after that, he bought the Logan House. Four generations of Kellys have owned and operated this tavern, which is another reason the building and business have survived.

John D. "Whiskers" Kelly had the gift of gab, which brought in his clientele and kept them coming. The Logan House became a center for Irish social life. During his tenure famous people stopped by: John L. Sullivan, world champion boxer; William F. "Buffalo Bill" Cody; and the infamous Al Capone. There was a dance hall on the second floor and a barbershop on the first floor operated by Victor Talmo for many years. Because of Hannah Kelly's financial prowess in the tavern's operation, the Kelly family was able to acquire much much of the property between DuPont and Union Streets along Delaware Avenue. Many Irish workers are reputed to have cashed their checks at the Logan House, where John D. Kelly Sr. sometimes had as much as $10,000 on hand.

---

[39] Barnard, *Forty Acres*, pp. 66-67;
Charles P. Wilson, "Fourth-Generation tavern owners renovate historic city taphouse", *Delaware Business Review*, Wilmington, DE, May 6-12, 1988, pp. 14, 19

Following World War I, John D. Kelly Jr. ran the tavern for his father until John D. Sr. died in 1938. The son rented it out to several proprietors, until a third generation Kelly, John D. Kelly III, a WWII U.S. Marine veteran, county sheriff, and later New Castle Register in Chancery and an amateur boxer, took over operation of the place in 1963. This Mr. Kelly initiated the tradition of the St. Patrick's Day parade in Wilmington in 1975 and the celebration that followed it at the Logan House.[40] Local resident and the author's fellow graduate of Wilmington High School, Walter Del Giorno, who frequented the Logan House in the 1960s, had this to say about Mr. Kelly, "He would greet and interact with the patrons then later do a monologue, which incorporated recognition of some of the patrons. He would often use their names but would invent some story about them. I was once introduced as 'Rocky' Del Giorno, an amateur boxer. I believe that Kelly's monologue always opened something like this, 'Good evening ladies and gentlemen and welcome to Kelly's Logan House overlooking the scenic ACME parking lot and the beautiful Wilmington Trolley Station.'" Mr. Kelly's children, Mary Ann and brother Michael, now run the Logan House which underwent renovation for the 100th anniversary of the site. Many Ann said at that time "I want people to love the Logan House just one fourth of what I do." They truly do. On July 7, 2006 movie star husband and wife Ryan Phillippe and Reese Witherspoon stopped by with family and friends. The Logan House is still THE gathering place on Delaware Avenue.[41]

The ACME grocery store and parking lot opposite the Logan House at the southwest corner of Delaware Avenue and DuPont Street was the site of the Baltimore & Ohio Railroad Station for the Baltimore & Philadelphia line going through Wilmington. The ornate red brick station completed in 1886 had two entrances on ground level, one on Delaware Avenue and one on DuPont Street, and steps led to the platform above. Among the services the Baltimore & Ohio station offered to the travelers on their line was a shoeshine stand run by John Vintigni for over thirty years. Mr. Vintigni's sons worked with him, and when they were not available he employed children from Siena Hall, a Catholic orphanage near the Delaware Art Museum. Gerald Vintigni related this information to Walt DelGiorno, who had these memories of the station. "Some-

---

[40]Barnard, p. 81;
Delaware Business Review, p. 14;
Gary Mullinax, "Tracks of Time," The News Journal, Wilmington, DE, 7 February, 1995, pp. D1
[41]E-mail interview with Walter Del Giorno, 13 February, 2004, Delaware Business Review, p. 14

times we went home to the Highlands via Delaware Avenue and cut through the tunnel that went under the tracks to the station. We were frequently chased out of there by the redcaps – the baggage handlers. A large grass and tree-lined park was adjacent to the station, stretching behind it to DuPont Street. We frequently played in that park and often slid down the grassy bank on cardboard to Fourteenth Street." Paul Schofield, whose family grew up on Delaware Avenue, remembers that this park had about fifty oak trees with stone walkways and a flagpole in the middle and that the Fourteenth Street side was banked all the way to the station.[42] The Baltimore & Ohio lunch counter at 1616 Delaware Avenue opened in the 1920s to serve the area. The Constantinou family bought this small sandwich shop in 1950, and operated it under that name until the Baltimore & Ohio station was razed in 1960. In 1923 the station sustained major damage due to fire, but it was restored to its vintage looks instead of being modernized. The last train ride on the Baltimore & Ohio line out of that station was Saturday, April 26, 1958 on the Old Blue Line, which made its run to Jersey City, New Jersey. Many residents of Forty Acres hopped on for the last ride. It was a sad day when the building was razed. Wilmington had lost a truly historic landmark.[43]

The end of the line for buses traveling Delaware Avenue was the car barn bordered by Delaware Avenue, DuPont and Clayton Streets and Gilpin Avenue, the same site where the electric trolleys were housed in the 1930s and 40s. The end of the car barn came in the 1960s, when it was demolished to make way for Trolley Square, a unique shopping center for Avenue residents, Forty Acres on one side and Happy Valley on the other. The center was built in 1978, a testament to change along the Avenue. Across the Avenue from Trolley Square on the south side, is the city's second and only surviving flatiron building, a four-story structure at 1600-1608 Delaware Avenue, which houses apartments and businesses. The 11,000 square foot brick building was constructed with two stories in 1921 by the American Guaranty Trust Company for only $9,500. Two more floors were added at some point, and the building has seen continued use since.[44] Before this building appeared on Delaware Avenue, there were other businesses within this block that served the neighborhood. One of these was Cappeau's Drugstore, built on the southeast corner of

---

[42] E-mail, Walter Del Giorno, 13-16, February, 2004

[43] Mullinax, "Tracks," p. D4;
Helping Hand, "Tracking down old memories," Sunday News Journal, 17 May 1987, p.H3

[44] Mullinax, "Tracks", p. D4

Delaware Avenue and DuPont Street in 1871. Trolley passengers would drop off prescriptions in the morning and pick them up on their way home. John Raskob, mentioned as the negotiator in the widening of Delaware Avenue, had his family's prescriptions filled there.. Cappeau's served as a gathering place for the youth of the neighborhood. Girls going out together often went to Cappeau's and sat at the pink marble soda fountain for a treat. A confectionary on Scott Street, Mrs. Black's, reputedly sold the best ice cream in the 1890s, but at Cappeau's one could get a vanilla or chocolate ice cream soda or a lime or lemon phosphate. Banana splits were more expensive but available to the adventurous. There were no booths at Cappeau's.[45]

Cappeau's drugstore is among the many buildings along Delaware Avenue which have met their demise. It was razed in 1967 and replaced by the Smoke Shop in 1973. The Smoke Shop was housed originally at 1620 Delaware Avenue where J.B. Connell had operated a cigar store as early as 1923. When the Constantinou family expanded their restaurant, the Smoke Shop moved to the corner. When Constantinou's, a fine restaurant in business for many years, moved to Union Street, Catherine Rooney's Irish pub took over the spot and is thriving. The building at 1622, which currently houses a liquor store, was a barber shop in 1923 operated by Nathan Bailey, then Betty Marie's beauty shop in 1934, and Zinnie's barber shop in the 1940s to 1950s, when it became a liquor store. Other businesses in the block included a dry cleaner at 1606 from the 1930s into the 1960s, and the Avenue deli at 1608 during the same time period. This section of Delaware Avenue, the Middle Depot/Trolley Square center of two neighborhoods, became the service hub for its residents. Further west along Delaware Avenue where the station park used to be is a car dealership. Across the street at 1707 is the long-running Del Rose Restaurant, originally a residence, and then the Terranova Tavern up to the 1960s. The restaurant next door to the Del Rose, Scratch MaGoo's, started out as a private residence and was later a barber shop, the third in the area, known as M.J. Haley's. By 1950 it was Mario's Restaurant, the Champagne Lounge by 1964 and a string of restaurants in between. The Blue Streak Gallery buildings at 1721 and 1723 were private homes as late as 1964.[46]

---

[45]Mullinax, "Tracks", p. D1;
Barnard, Forty Acres, pp. 117-118;
Letter, John J. Raskob to T.H. Cappeau, 26 September 1935;
Accession 473 File 33a
[46]Mullinax, "Tracks", p.D4

The development of the Forty Acres neighborhood is thoroughly covered by Mary Ann Barnard in her University of Delaware thesis of 1981. As Ms. Barnard states, most of the land in the area bounded by Delaware Avenue and Lovering Avenue, and DuPont and Union Streets had been subdivided into small plots to make them available to workingmen moving into the area. "In some blocks the houses were built right to the sidewalk; in others front porches would be between the sidewalk and the house. And some houses even had small front yards." Except along the Avenue, this residential neighborhood has changed very little in 100 years.[47]

Supporting institutions in the Forty Acres included a grocery store, a bakery, a church, schools, a fire station and liquor stores. The Scott Quarry at the intersection of what is now Delaware Avenue and Union Street provided employment for many during its operation into the early 1900s. Walt Del Giorno remembers that as late as 1957 the American Grocery Store operated where the Delaware Avenue Liquors is now and where the quarry had been. A bakery at the corner of Lincoln Street and Gilpin Avenue, run by the Taylor family for many years, was a favorite meeting place. There were three schools in this area. Mr. Del Giorno recalls that Public School #27 near the top of the hill from the mills near Rockford Park served grades 4 and 5. Public School #13, located south of Delaware Avenue on Union Street, served grades 1-3 and grade 6. St. Ann's Roman Catholic Church opened a school in 1899 for 1st to 8th graders. It was the only school within Forty Acres. Those who continued their education went to Wilmington High School up into the 1930s. Public School #13 building still stands and serves as offices. St. Ann's also opened a commercial school in 1905 for 8th grade graduates who desired training for clerical and business jobs in the city. St. Ann's was one of the principal churches serving the area.[48]

St. Ann's Roman Catholic Church was built in Forty Acres in 1888, replacing St. James Church on Lovering Avenue and DuPont Streets, the foundations of which were weakened by the vibrations of trains on the Baltimore & Ohio tracks running nearby. By 1894 the Catholic population in the area had swelled to 2,000 parishioners. In 1933 the rectory at St. Ann's was built, and the twenty-eight steps leading up to the entrance were removed in 1935, making the basement floor level with the main entrance to the church. John Raskob, the

---

[47] Barnard, *Forty Acres*, pp. 92, 122

[48] E-mail, Walter Del Giorno, 27 February 2004;
Barnard, *Forty Acres*, pp. 69-70. 119-122;
Marianna McLaughlin, "St. Ann's Standing Tall at age 100", *The Dialog*, Wilmington, DE, 24 July 1987, p. 1, 6

DuPont Company executive mentioned earlier, had eleven children, and they were all members of the parish. Other churches serving this Delaware Avenue residential area were Immanuel Episcopal Church on Riverview and Mt. Salem Methodist Church on Nineteenth Street bordering Rockford Park. The only fire company to locate in Forty Acres was the Water Witch Fire Engine Company No. 5. Originally located in the city, it closed in the 1880s as more fire companies formed. On April 12, 1893, the Water Witch was reorganized in Forty Acres, and built a three-story building with a tower housing a one-thousand pound bell on Gilpin Avenue just west of Scott Street. This fire company has been serving the neighborhood ever since. Extensive renovations to preserve the fire house, currently called Fire Station No. 5, were carried out in 1987 at a cost of $435,000 by Shelly's of Delaware. A museum is housed on the second floor.[49]

---

[49] *The Dialog*, P. 6;
Barnard, *Forty Acres*, p. 119;
"Fire Station #5 renovation," *State Chamber News*, 18 November 1987, p. 33

Aerial view of Delaware Avenue
between Clayton and DuPont Streets.
The car barn, Logan House
and the Baltimore & Ohio railroad station
can all be seen in this view, 1939

Dallin Collection
Courtesy Hagley Mesuem and Library.

Delaware Avenue - Bethany Baptist Church
at Lincoln Street, Wilmington, Delaware, 1900.

Courtesy University of Delaware Special Collections.

Chapter Five
Union to Greenhill Avenue

Joshua T. Heald, the real estate developer of Happy Valley and Forty Acres, went on to develop the Brinkle property between Union Street and Brandywine Park in the 1880s. He had been made agent for the disposition of the Brinkle property in 1880, as he had for the Lovering property in 1860. He developed this property by promoting it as a 'fine residential area.' It grew slowly but steadily into a community known as the Highlands and was incorporated into the city limits in 1895. In this neighborhood, the homes on the north side along Delaware Avenue were built along the lines of country mansions. More modest housing on the south side of the Highlands was purchased by middle-class families. A member of the Dougherty family bought a home in the Highlands on Seventeenth Street, but in 1888 moved to Forty Acres on Lincoln Street in order to be closer to St. Ann's.[50]

One house of note northwest of Union Street on Delaware Avenue is number 2021. This house belonged to Pierre S. du Pont (1870-1954), President of the DuPont Company during World War I and the man responsible for widening Delaware Avenue. Mr. du Pont, who rented this house to his cousin Victor du Pont Jr. (1852-1911) and his wife Josephine from 1895 to 1906 for $28 a month, sold it to Victor in 1906. Letters between Victor and Pierre during these years provide insight into everyday life then. On October 18, 1895 Victor writes complaining of a leak which the next door neighbor, Mr. Zehn, "says was caused by the pipes freezing last winter." Victor was

---

[50] Barnard, *Forty Acres*, pp. 39, 120-123

not moving in for a week or so, but he urged Pierre to get a plumber, "plumbers are so uncertain it is well to give them plenty of time." Pierre had "Brison" do the work. On September 18, 1896 Victor writes Pierre reminding him that during the previous winter, when they had to keep the refrigerator (ice box?) in the yard because of the heat from the furnace, that it was regularly broken into and "we lost 3 Sunday dinners besides other things." Victor asks Pierre to have a shed built around it as security, which Pierre did. In the same letter, Victor complains of falling plaster, but says the shed is more important. The following spring the plaster is repaired and the walls are covered over in wallpaper. Extensive wallpapering was done throughout the house in 1898, and letters between August and November cover Josephine's choice of patterns. In 1902 the kitchen floor was raised two inches and a cement walk was laid out around the yard. Paul Schofield, current resident of the house across the street, thought that T. Coleman du Pont (1863-1930), President of the newly formed DuPont Company in 1902, also lived in this house. T. Coleman du Pont may very well have lived there for a time after Victor died, but his main house was in the 800 block of Broom St.[51]

An elementary school in the Highlands opened in 1953 with the closure of Public School #13. Walt Del Giorno remembers this about the school: "Highlands was a large, new school with extensive playground areas. There were swings and a merry-go-round on the lower part, which was grass and dirt. The large macadam area included a basketball court on which we usually played dodge ball." Mr. DelGiorno talked about the safety patrol, which helped students cross the streets. He served on the Honor Guard of the Safety Patrol in 6th grade and "proudly wore my captain's badge on my white safety patrol belt."[52]

In 1889 William Bancroft and his wife deeded forty-eight acres to Wilmington, thus establishing Rockford Park at the end of Delaware Avenue. Ten years later a water tower to furnish "water supply to the highlands" was built as it became necessary to build a "high service reservoir." The tower, constructed in Rockford Park on the highest point in the city, was

---

[51] *Letters between Victor duPont Jr. and Pierre S. du Pont, 18 October 1895, 20 October 1895, 18 Sept. 1896; 8 May 1897, 27 April 1897, 17 August 1898, 23 July 1902, 26 August 1902, 22 August 1902, 27 December 1902, 29 March 1904, 24 July 1905, 30 August 1906, 13 July 1906, from the Papers of Pierre S. du Pont, Longwood Manuscripts, Group 10 Series A File 272 Box 209 Hagley Museum and Library;*
Letters between Pierre S. du Pont and William K. duPont, 15 August 1898, 26 August 1898, 21 September 1898, 24 September 1898, 29 September 1898; 23 November 1898 and 6 November 1898, LMSS 10/A/File 20 Box 15, Hagley Museum and Library
[52] *E-mail, Walter Del Giorno, 13 February 2004*

fifty-seven feet in diameter and seventy-five feet high with a tile roof. It was opened to the public in 1903. The Highlands Community Council, of which Mr. Maurice du Pont Lee (1885-1974) was an active member, had a picture of the Rockford Tower on its letterhead in 1964. The boundaries of the Highlands are also given: Pennsylvania Avenue to Brandywine Creek; Baltimore & Ohio Railroad to Rising Sun Lane. One of the issues of concern for the Council in 1964 was the changing of bus routes. The Highlands then encompassed the Logan House, the Baltimore & Ohio Station, Forty Acres and St. Ann's. In 1910 the Highlands area was a desirable place to live and life was pleasant there. That feeling is just as current in the twenty-first century. Good restaurants and unique stores are within walking distance of homes. There is a quaintness in the character of the area, and the architecture of historic buildings and residences draws people to live there. Easy access to downtown is another factor. It's a village within a city with its history intact.[53]

So, Delaware Avenue, where do you take us from here?

---

[53]Barnard, *Forty Acres*, p. 122;
History of Buildings in the Highlands, Prepared by the Highlands Community Council, Wilmington, DE, no date. Letters between Hugh B. Horning, President of the Highlands Community Council and Maurice duPont Lee, 19 May 1964, Maurice duPont Lee Papers, Accession 1452 Box 35, Hagley Museum and Library; The Newsletter of The Highlands Community Council, April 1964 and June 1964, Accession 1452 Box 35, Hagley Museum and Library

1887 map showing Happy Valley
and part of Forty Acres from Geo. Baist's
Atlas of the City of Wilmington.

Courtesy Hagley Museum and Library.

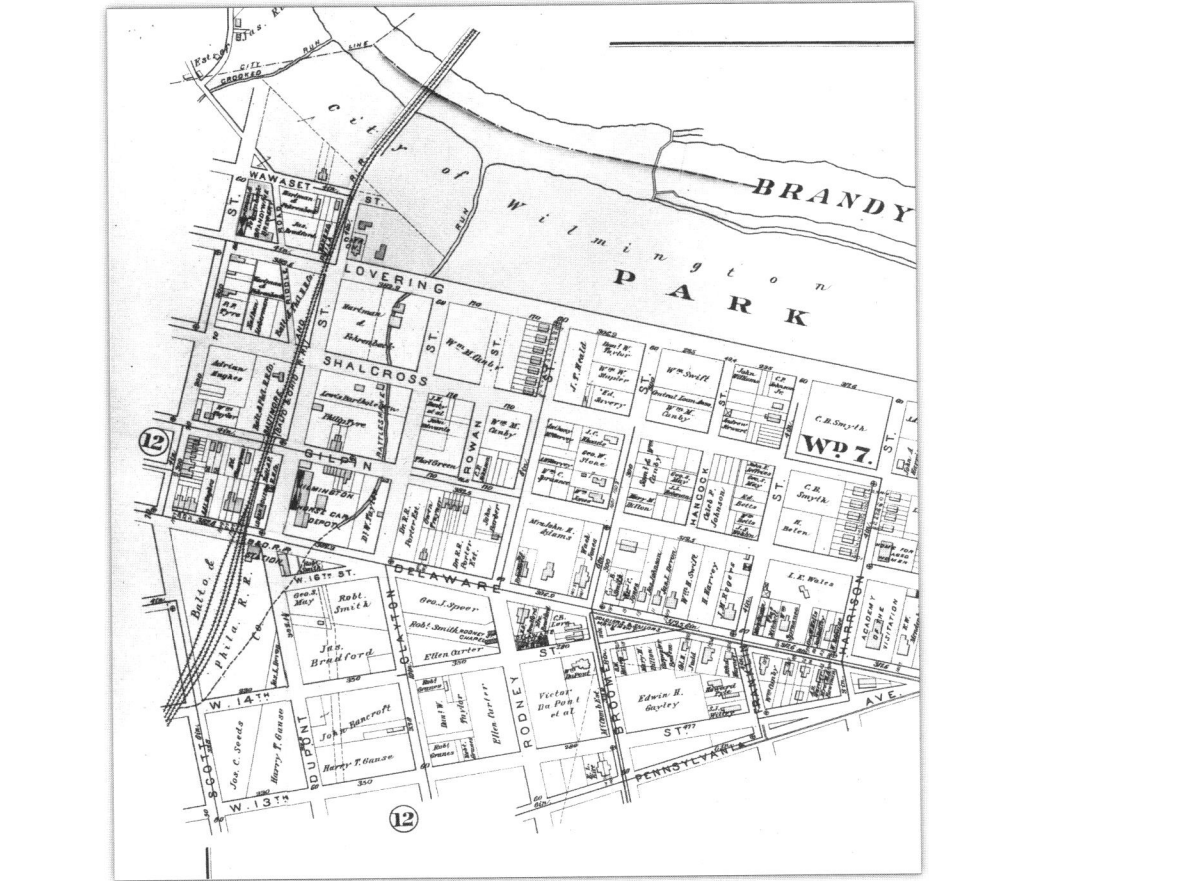

Railroad bridge over the Brandywine River, 1915.

Courtesy Hagley Museum and Library.

Acknowledgements

I started research on this history of Delaware Avenue over two years ago. During the process of research and writing, I have benefited from the memories and help of a number of people. First of all I would like to thank my colleagues at the Hagley Musuem and Library. Without the help of Marsha Mills Warwick, this work would not have seen the light of day. Marsha typed and revised the manuscript from my handwritten copy at least four times; my home computer was unfortunately "on the fritz". Hats off to Marsha.

Richard James and Jon Williams both scanned the illustrations used in this book for me, a few of them at the last minute, so thank you Richard and Jon. I want to thank my Wilmington High School classmate, Walter Del Giorno for his enthusiastic and detailed memories of the Logan House, the train station and Highlands school. I am very much indebted to Mary Ann Kelly, part owner of the Kelly Logan House, for taking time to tell me the history of her family and the tavern, and to show me the amazing historical documents on display there. I also want to thank my good friends and long time residents of Wilmington, Delaware—Ruth Kolber, Jean Lyons, and Paul Schofield—for their memories as well. One last person I would like to thank is Gordon Pfeiffer for letting me use some of his post cards from his wonderful collection in my book.

Marjorie G. McNinch

BIBLIOGRAPHY

Barnard, Mary Ann. *A History of Forty Acres to 1910: Myth and Reality in a Wilmington, Delaware Neighborhood.* Newark, DE: University of Delaware, 1981.

Baist, G. Wm. *Atlas of the city of Wilmington, Delaware and vicinity.* Philadelphia: G.W. Baist, 1887.

Beers, D. G. *Atlas of the state of Delaware from actual surveys by and under the direction of D. G. Beers.* Philadelphia: Pomeroy & Beers, 1868.

Conrad, Henry Clay. *History of the state of Delaware from the earliest settlements to the year 1907.* Wilmington, DE: Author, 1907.

Cox, Harold E. *Diamond State Trolleys.* Forty Fort, PA: Harold E. Cox, 1991.

Delaware Housing Commission. *Report of the Housing Commission of the State of Delaware,* December 1932, Dover, DE: 1933

Every Evening. *History of Wilmington: the commercial social and religious growth of the City during the past century.* Wilmington, DE: F.T. Smiley, 1894

Federal Writers' Project of the Works Progress Administration for the State of Delaware. *Delaware, A Guide to the First State.* American Guide Series. Sponsored by Edward W. Cooch, Lieutenant Governor. New York: The Viking Press, 1938

Henry, Allen J., editor. *Life of Alexis Irenee du Pont.* Philadelphia: Wm. F. Fell Co., 1945

The Highlands Community Council. "A History of Building in the Highlands." Wilmington, DE: The Highlands Community Council, 1965.

Historical and Biographical Encyclopedia of Delaware. Wilmington, DE: Aldine Publishing and Engraving Co., 1882

Hoffecker, Carol E. *Wilmington, Delaware: Portrait of an Industrial City, 1830-1910*. Virginia: University Press of Virginia for the Eleutherian Mills-Hagley Foundation, 1974.

Jones, Theophilus K., "Recollections of Wilmington from 1845 to 1860." Chapter 52, Vol. 5 Historical and Biographical Papers, Wilmington, DE: Historical Society of Delaware, 1909, 5 volumes.

Lincoln, Anna T. *Wilmington, Delaware: Three Centuries Under Four Flags, 1609-1937*. Rutland, VT: The Tuttle Publishing Company, Inc., 1937

McNinch, Marjorie G. *Festivals*. Wilmington, DE: Cedar Tree Books, Ltd., 1997

McNinch, Marjorie G. *Silver Screen*. Wilmington, DE: Cedar Tree Books, Ltd., 1997

McNinch, Marjorie G. *Wilmington in Vintage Postcards*. Postcard History Series. Charleston, SC: Arcadia Publishing, 2002.

Montgomery, Elizabeth. *Reminiscences of Wilmington, In Familiar Village Tales*. Philadelphia: T.K. Collins, 1981.

Rapp, William F. "Notes on Delaware Street and Interurban Railways, 1900-1912." *The Railway History Monograph*, Volume III No. 2, April 1974. Crete, Nebraska: J-B Publishing Company, 1974

Reed, H. Clay, editor. *Delaware: A History of the First State*. 2 volumes. New York: Lewis Historical Publishing Company, Inc., 1947

Scharf, J. Thomas. *History of Delaware, 1609-1888*. 2 volumes. Philadelphia: L.J. Richards & Co., 1888

Wilkinson, Norman *The Brandywine Home Front during the Civil War, 1861-1865*. Wilmington, DE: Kaumagraph Co., 1966

Wilmington, Delaware. Broadside. 1869 advertisement for sale of lots on Delaware Avenue. Broadside, 1869

Zebley, Frank R. *The Churches of Delaware*. Wilmington, DE: 1947.

Newspapers and magazines

AAA World magazine, March/April 2004

Delaware Business Review, Wilmington, DE, 1988.

The Dialog, Wilmington, DE, 1987.

Every Evening newspaper, Wilmington, DE, 1919

Evening Journal newspaper, Wilmington, DE, 1992, 1995, 1996, 1997, 2004, 2005, 2006

State Chamber News newspaper, Dover, DE, 1987

Manuscripts

Wallace Carothers papers, Accession 1842, Hagley Museum and Library.

Henry B. du Pont Papers, Accession 1608, Hagley Museum and Library.

Pierre S. du Pont Papers, Longwood Manuscripts Group 10 Series A., Hagley Museum and Library.

DuPont Company Public Affairs Dept. records, Accession 1410, Hagley Museum and Library.

Jasper E. Crane Papers, Accession 1417, Hagley Museum and Library.

John J. Raskob Papers, Accession 473, Hagley Museum and Library.

Maurice du Pont Lee Papers, Accession 1452, Hagley Museum and Library.

Spruance/Lea Family Papers, Accession 1114, Hagley Museum and Library.

P. S. du Pont Photographic Collection, HML.

Dallin Aerial Photograph Collection, HML

Postcard Collection, Special Collections, University of Delaware

Historical Society of Delaware Photograph Collection

Interviews By Author

Walter DelGiorno through e-mail correspondence, February 2004.

Ruth Kolber and Jean Lyons, March 2004.

Paul Schofield, May and September 2006.